The Indisputable Guide to SEO Success

SCOTT ORTH

Cover Design by PriscillaPowers.com

ISBN: 057816504X
ISBN-13: 978-0578165042

CONTENTS

INTRODUCTION

Let's cut to the chase. You don't have time to read and sift through 200+ pages of instructions to get your business noticed. Instead, you need to be told exactly what to do in a short, step-by-step guide for success.

This guide is purposely light on pages, but extremely heavy on value. The goal is for you to understand the exact process to succeed in SEO in one short read – and then to easily implement each process on your own, through my detailed examples within each step. My methods are tried and true, using proven Google approved best-practices.

THE FACTS AS I SEE THEM

I've been creating SEO success for over 16 years… nearly half my life. I worked on SEO before "SEO" was a thing, and definitely before it was a service or a profession.

I created my career by convincing a web agency that they needed me on board for what was coming in a new age of website marketing. The timing was good. The market blossomed and I doubled my income every year for 4 years straight because of this "new marketing method".

I've been around since the beginning of Google. I've lived through every single algorithm change and update, seen just about everything one could possibly see regarding SEO, from the good to the horrible and everything in between. I've done more trial and error experiments than I could ever hope to count, built a hundred of my own websites just to test theories, blew through a few hosting accounts after being banned or kicked off for spam (you gotta learn the good and the bad to truly know what works), and I spent the better part of 6 years going to every search and marketing conference possible, listening to, questioning, and debating with colleagues as well as search engine representative's from Google and Bing.

I've worked on every kind, type, structure, and format of website in a long list of industries; Business to Business, Business to Consumer, brochure, lead generation, and e-commerce.

I've failed a thousand times; but succeeded 10 times more often.

I am an SEO Expert!

So what is my point? It's simple… If you disagree with the following guide to SEO success, then you've obviously not been around long enough, seen or witnessed enough, or been through the ringer enough to know what you're talking about. They are, quite simply, indisputable.

- If you believe a keyword in the domain name no longer matters… you're wrong
- If you believe H1 header tags are no longer all that meaningful… you're wrong

1

- If you believe the Keyword Meta tag doesn't matter… you're wrong
- If you believe Pay-per-Click and other traffic sources don't matter for organic success… you're wrong

The above issues, as well as dozens of others, have all been stated by search engine representatives… most notably those from Google. And yet I can prove the importance of every single one through consistent client success stories from 1999 through today.

One of the first things you need to know to be successful in SEO is to believe what works through your own tests and trials, and only listen to search engine reps, news sites, and other search marketers with half-an-ear… because at least 50% of what you're being told is complete garbage and is based on rumors and misinformation.

So let's get to it. The Indisputable Guide to SEO Success…

I may reference Google often herein. Know that everything I advise is for search engines in general; but that Google is the most important and therefore gets all the mentions here.

Google has stated for years "Build your website for your users, not for search engines". This made sense a dozen years ago, and it still makes sense today. When you think through the most user-friendly scenario of how your website could be structured, you'll end up with a site that is pretty much already optimized for search engines.

Follow these steps and you're sure to gain SEO success. Depending on the level of competitiveness in your industry, you may need to go into even greater detail in your work, as well as branch out to more extensive off-site SEO. But these steps will help most companies get much further than they are today in their organic ranking success.

If you consistently apply the steps below, and revisit them week after week (as necessary), you will gain great SEO success.

In my examples below we will assume work on a website that sells Wibbles - my example site, www.UnitedWibbles.com. But keep in mind, whether you're a product business or service business, the theories work exactly the same.

I'll walk you through each step, but the overall premise of the entire process is to create a theme based website, with individually themed pages, each page with its own very specific topic (or theme). Everything then revolves around this theme structure as you'll see through this guide.

For regular updates and tips, sign up by texting **SEOGUIDE** *to* **22828** *or by Scanning our QR Code:*

If after reading this guide you still need assistance, ThriveSearch.com offers full service online marketing services and training at every level (startup to enterprise and everything in-between). Contact for rates to help you succeed.

STEP 1: KEYWORD RESEARCH

The first thing you need to do in order to understand your keywords is to do a little keyword research. It doesn't matter if you think you already know the words for your business. Do the research anyway.

You might be surprised what great little gold nuggets you can uncover. But even if nothing mind-boggling comes out of it, you can be sure that you'll end up with a list of keywords and how popular they are in search. This is very important data for keyword planning.

Years ago I had a prospective client tell me that they had no need to hire me because their current agency had already gotten them twenty #1 keywords (keywords that displayed their website listing in the first spot (top of page) of Google) and they couldn't be happier, because they had only two #1 keywords before hiring them.

I asked them which keywords. Filled with pride, they gave the list of keywords to me. I researched and found that all twenty #1 ranked keywords received an average of 12 monthly searches (globally).

Not so proud anymore, they gave me their analytics access. I was able to determine that after six months of having these twenty #1 ranked keywords, they had never received one single visit from them.

Needless to say, they hired me. Six months later we achieved 43 top 10 rankings. Only 7 of which were #1's – yet those 7 #1 rankings drove over 1,800 monthly visits to their website. Keyword research – It tells you what words people will actually use. Don't skip this step!

Use Google Keyword Planner
Start by going to www.google.com/adwords and sign up for an account. It's free, and you don't need to actually run an ad campaign. We're just interested in the keyword tool and data at this point.

Once in the account, go to "Tools" at the top left of navigation and choose 'Keyword Planner'.

In the keyword planner you can use the tool a few different ways to find keywords. Follow the instructions on the page to move through the process.

Q Find new keywords

▼ Search for new keywords using a phrase, website or category

Enter one or more of the following:
Your product or service

For example, flowers or used cars

Your landing page

www.example.com/page

Your product category

Enter or select a product category

Targeting ?		Customize your search ?	
All locations		Keyword filters	
All languages		Keyword options	
Google		Show broadly related ideas	
Negative keywords		Hide keywords in my account	
		Hide keywords in my plan	
Date range ?			
Show avg. monthly searches for: Last 12 months		Keywords to include	

Get ideas

Be sure to export the keyword data into Excel. I like to export, then go back into the tool and search a couple more variations. Export to Excel each time. Once you're done, combine all Excel sheets and run the deduplication tool (under 'Data' in Excel) to remove all duplications.

You'll then be left with a complete list of keyword data to base your website content planning on.

With this list of keywords, you can then assign appropriate keywords to each of your website pages.

In my example we're selling Wibbles. So if one of my keywords is 'blue wobbly wibbles', then I want to assign that keyword to a page on my website that is all about blue wobbly wibbles. Seems simple, right?

STEP 2: PAGE AND NAVIGATION HIERARCHY

Now that we have our keyword list, we want to look at planning our pages for www.unitedwibbles.com. With the keyword export from Google, we now know what people are searching on when looking for information about wibbles, and which keywords are more frequently searched than others.

Here is our initial keyword list that we want to target (obviously I have shortened this list so I can just give you the direct examples for success):

Wibbles
Blue Wibbles
Green Wibbles
Wibbles under my bed
Wobbly Wibbles
Straight wibbles

Depending on your focus, your list may be 10 words long or 5,000 words long. Your goal will be to find the primary keywords that make the most sense for your business.

In our list, we have mostly specific, product type keywords; but also with an odd one here and there (i.e. "wibbles under my bed"). These types of keywords are great for content pages or blog posts, if they don't fit perfectly into your default page structure.

Based on our 6 primary keywords above, our page structure, or navigation hierarchy, might start to look something like this:

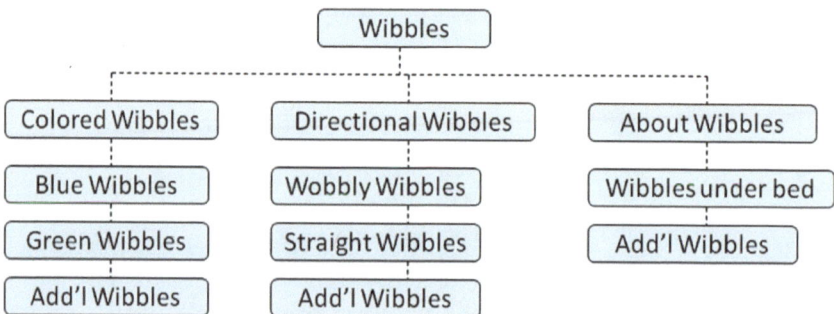

The Google Trio of SEO

The first three most important elements for SEO on Google are:

- URL page name and structure
- Page title
- H1 header tag

If the three items above are themed appropriately, then Google knows exactly what this page is about, and all that is left is supporting the theme with appropriate content, images, videos, and related links.

STEP 3: URL PAGE NAME CONVENTION

As mentioned, the URL itself is one of the first elements Google sees, and based on what the page name is, Google will be looking for a theme of the page.

You want to use a clean URL structure. Think of it like a folder directory structure. You've seen this sort of structure whenever you look for a file on your computer:

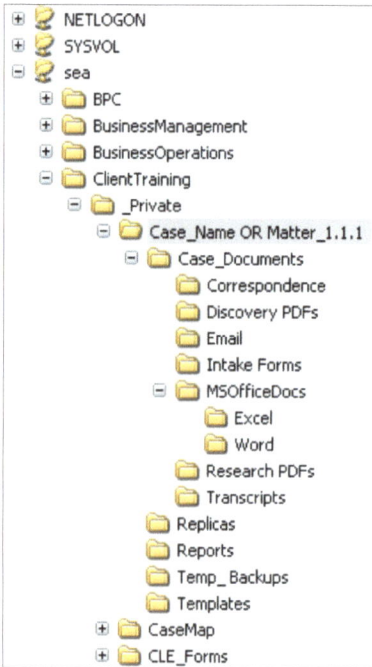

NETLOGON
SYSVOL
sea
  BPC
  BusinessManagement
  BusinessOperations
  ClientTraining
    _Private
      Case_Name OR Matter_1.1.1
        Case_Documents
          Correspondence
          Discovery PDFs
          Email
          Intake Forms
          MSOfficeDocs
            Excel
            Word
          Research PDFs
          Transcripts
        Replicas
        Reports
        Temp_Backups
        Templates
      CaseMap
      CLE_Forms

A website is built in the same kind of structure. You just need to name the "folders" correctly so that Google matches them to your keyword focus.

Thus our Wibbles structure might look like this in folder view:

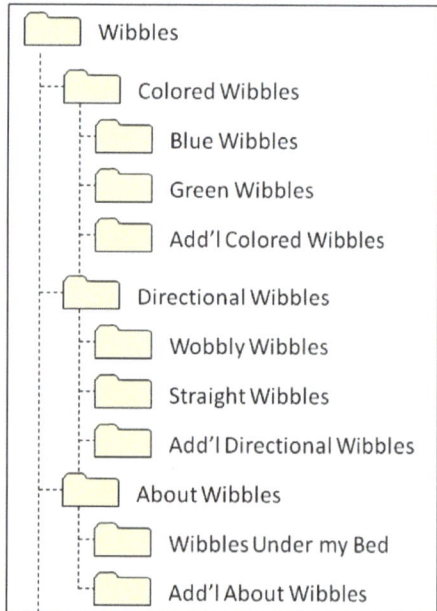

Wibbles
  Colored Wibbles
    Blue Wibbles
    Green Wibbles
    Add'l Colored Wibbles
  Directional Wibbles
    Wobbly Wibbles
    Straight Wibbles
    Add'l Directional Wibbles
  About Wibbles
    Wibbles Under my Bed
    Add'l About Wibbles

If you took these folders and formatted each for a horizontal view, they would like this:

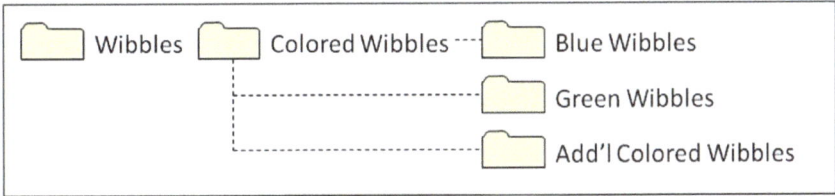

From this view, you can simply turn them into URLs as shown here (where the main Wibbles directory turns into your domain name):

www.UnitedWibbles.com/colored-wibbles
www.UnitedWibbles.com/colored-wibbles/blue-wibbles
www.UnitedWibbles.com/colored-wibbles/green-wibbles
www.UnitedWibbles.com/colored-wibbles/addl-colored-wibbles

Here's another way to look at it, using just 'Blue Wibbles' as an example:

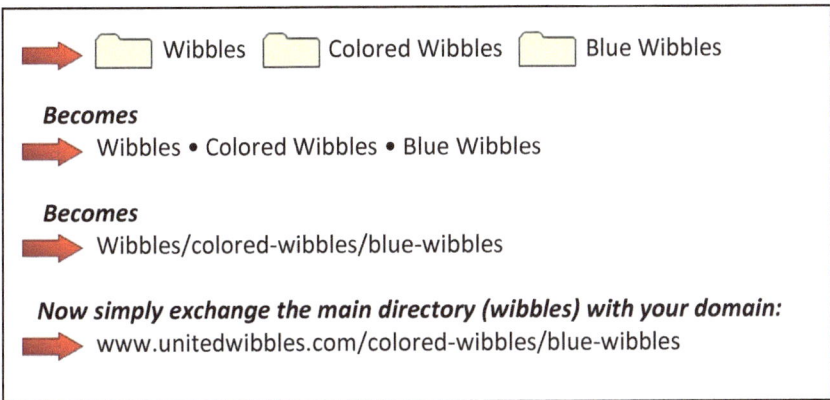

This is the 'perfect' URL structure in the eyes of Google. Not only does it follow a logical directory format, which Google is based on; but it also follows a logical sequence of page and category theming (i.e. colors vs. directional… blue vs. green).

(**Note:** always use hyphens to separate words. Some argue it doesn't matter, but hyphens have been the proven go-to method since Google first launched. So stick with it).

Think about this logical URL structure when building a content plan for your website. If planned appropriately, the URLs will create a logical hierarchy of pages. Exactly what users… and Google… want to see.

Based on this method, we can now take each of our pages from our sitemap framework and assign the appropriate URL to each page, giving us our optimized URL structure across the website. Examples below:

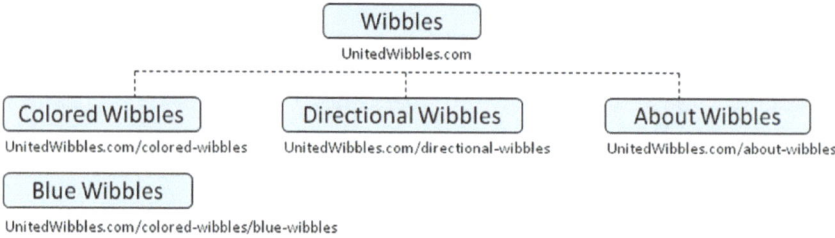

```
                    ┌──────────────────┐
                    │     Wibbles      │
                    └──────────────────┘
                      UnitedWibbles.com
     ┌────────────────────────┼────────────────────────┐
┌──────────────────┐  ┌──────────────────┐  ┌──────────────────┐
│  Colored Wibbles │  │ Directional Wibbles│ │  About Wibbles   │
└──────────────────┘  └──────────────────┘  └──────────────────┘
UnitedWibbles.com/colored-wibbles  UnitedWibbles.com/directional-wibbles  UnitedWibbles.com/about-wibbles

┌──────────────────┐
│   Blue Wibbles   │
└──────────────────┘
UnitedWibbles.com/colored-wibbles/blue-wibbles
```

NOTE: If you change any current URLs you have on your website, make sure you install 301 redirects. These redirects tell search engines that the old URL has moved to a new location (new URL). Without 301 redirects, your old URLs, and any history you've gained with them on search engines, will simply disappear forever.

If you're working with new URLs or a new domain, no need to worry about these redirects.

Installing 301 redirects may be quite different depending on your website coding language and/or Content Management System. Google "301 redirects <insert your CMS or code language>" or talk to your web admin or host provider for more help with these.

If after reading this guide you still need assistance, ThriveSearch.com offers full service online marketing services and training at every level (startup to enterprise and everything in-between). Contact for rates to help you succeed.

STEP 4: TITLES AND HEADER TAGS

Remember the Google Trio of SEO I mentioned? Titles and H1 Header tags are the second and third components of that.

Now that you have each page named, you have the keyword assigned, and your URL is structured; next you want to match your keyword optimized page name to your Page Title and H1 Header Tag. Let's look at Page Title first.

There are two parts to an optimized title:
1. Your themed keyword, which will be a repeat of your page name
2. Your brand. This comes at the end of the title

Hundreds of our own tests over the years have proven time and time again that you want to put your keyword first in your title (as far to the left as possible), and then end your title with your brand.

Ending the title with your brand gives you an opportunity to connect every single page to your brand, as well as show your brand prominently in search results.

We usually use the pipe "|" as the separator between your keyword and your brand mention. Therefore, an example Page Title for our Green Wibbles page would be:

Green Wibbles | United Wibbles

Let's say our actual company name is United Wibbles of the World, we can simply change the title to:

Green Wibbles | United Wibbles of the World

You want to be careful about Title length though. Your title should always be under 55 characters to ensure maximum display opportunities. Knowing this, it's best to shorten the brand section of your title as much as possible so that you give more room for longer keywords.

As an example, let's say we have a page focused on 'Green Wobbly Wibbles'. That's already 20 characters. Adding the pipe and our longer brand name above would put us over 55 characters. This means in some cases our title will be truncated, or cut off at the end. Getting cut off isn't the end of the world, but why wouldn't you want your entire message and brand name to show? Just makes sense to keep it under 55 characters.

Keep the brand portion as short as your brand allows; giving more space for keywords in the beginning of the title.

Your H1 Header tag will be your title up to the pipe (or separator). In the example above, our H1 tag would then be:

Green Wibbles

You can slightly change this if it makes sense for your page. I might say 'Green Wibbles Description' or 'Buy Green Wibbles'; but in most cases it works best to simply repeat the Page Title up to the separator.

TIP: You should only have one H1 tag on a page. Never more than one. NEVER! Use sub-headers (H2, H3, H4) for additional header needs on a page.

Google Trio Summary:
By following the steps above, you now have a perfectly themed trio as follows:

Page Name or URL Name: /green-wibbles
Page Title: Green Wibbles | United Wibbles
H1 Header: Green Wibbles

STEP 5: THEME MATCHED CONTENT

You've got your theme. The page is about Green Wibbles. Is it a product page? A description page? A FAQ page? Whatever the page's purpose, simply make sure you follow that theme.

I don't get hung up on ratios like some people. Some feel that you should make sure your keyword is between 2% and 4% of your content density, but not above 4% or you'll get penalized, etc… Bleh!

My success has come from using common sense. Google scans every bit of content on a page. That means if every page has standard information in the header, footer, or elsewhere… like your phone number, a tagline, maybe a marketing message of some sort… all of that text is scanned and reviewed (not just the 'content' section of the page). So there is some level of truth that if you only mention 'green wibbles' one time on a page that has 500 words, it's not doing much to support the intended theme.

But conversely, you don't want to repeat your keyword over and over ad nauseam either. It will offend your visitors, as well as Google.

Example of bad themed content:

> You've found the best green wibbles site around. At United Wibbles our green wibbles are better than any other green wibbles you'll find out there. In fact, other green wibbles can't match up to our green wibbles, because we make our green wibbles in a special green wibble factory.

Yes, in theory, the above content supports the theme of the page. But it's hard to read and will almost certainly be flagged by Google for keyword spam.

Example of good themed content:

> We believe you will find that our Green Wibbles are the best available for purchase. Our family has been in the business of making Wibbles for more than 50 years. Our green color is the most popular; though we offer Wibbles in 14 other colors as well. We trust you will absolutely love your purchase!

Note in the above content we said 'green wibbles' but we also simply said 'wibbles' and also 'green' in separate sentences. This is a good content method as it makes the content more natural and readable, but Google will connect instances of both 'green' and 'wibbles' to support the theme of the page as well.

STEP 6: OPTIMIZED META DESCRIPTION

Meta Descriptions will not improve how you rank, so some might say they don't belong in the Indisputable guide to SEO Success. But those people... would be wrong! Success is not just showing up on a search page. Success is getting traffic and obtaining your goals through your SEO efforts. So let's discuss Meta Descriptions.

The Meta Description is your marketing message that goes along with your page title. There are a couple things to consider when developing your Description:

- It should be less than 160 characters so that your full message gets displayed and not truncated.
- It should use your keyword once... maybe twice
- It should be unique on every page, with a message focused on that particular page's theme
- It should work as a marketing message to entice someone to click on your listing (think of it like an ad you want people to act on)

We know from our work in Step 4 that the listing title for the page we were working on will be:

Green Wibbles | United Wibbles

We'll want to keep that in mind as we write our description. An example might be:

"At United Wibbles we offer the highest quality Green Wibbles available. Buy now and receive free shipping and a 90-day quality guarantee."

<Note: Google auto-bolds any match of a search query. If someone searches for 'green wibbles' then every instance of 'green' and 'wibbles' in your entire listing/ad will be bolded>

With the work we've done in the steps above, our organic listing (or ad) will now show up on Google. If the search query was 'Buy green wibbles', our listing would look like this:

Green Wibbles | United **Wibbles**

www.united**wibbles**.com/colored-**wibbles**/**green-wibbles**

At United **Wibbles** we offer the highest quality **Green Wibbles** available.
Buy now and receive free shipping and a 90-day quality guarantee.

STEP 7: META KEYWORD TAG

This is a very simple step. Many SEO folks recommend skipping the keyword tag. That's not a good idea. It seems to be true that the tag is not used by Google for SEO; however, we know that it absolutely is used by both Google's and Bing's pay-per-click algorithm as a way to track ad relevance and improve ad quality score.

The tag is also used by smaller search engines and search directories. It's a simple addition, and it has some level of purpose, so don't exclude it.

An optimized Keyword Tag will list only the most related keywords and variations for its intended page (following the theme), and should include no more than 10 keywords or phrases (separated by commas). Just like with the theme of a page, you want to keep this tag focused on its actual theme. More than 10 keywords dilute the tag, and is therefore frowned upon by search engines (note: each term or phrase between commas counts as one keyword).

For our Green Wibbles page, the tag might look like this:

Meta Keywords: green wibbles, wibbles, tall green wibbles (note: this is only 3 keywords)

There's not much more to the tag than that. You can add secondary focused terms if it's appropriate, but be sure to keep it to a maximum of 10 terms/phrases.

STEP 8: CANONICAL URL

If you've completed all 7 steps above, across all the major pages of your website, you're done with page-level SEO. Just a couple steps more and you're done with all the most important page-level SEO work that can be done on your website.

'Canonical' is rooted in the meaning of order, or following a usual order. For our purposes, it just means you want one single URL for a page. Any duplicate URLs will either be discounted or could harm your rankings due to duplicate content penalties. There are several ways we can use canonical tags and URL's; but here we're just focusing on the most primary use only.

Typically by default, a host server is setup to display your pages with and without www. – Thus our home page can be found at both:

http://www.UnitedWibbles.com AND at http://UnitedWibbles.com

This is a bad thing because Google sees the two URLs above as completely separate and unique. Therefore, you want to set your domain to use a canonical URL. It doesn't matter which of the above you want (with www or without www), you simply need to choose one and make it your canonical URL.

Done correctly, it will also auto-redirect people to the Canonical version you chose. For instance, if you choose to go *without* www. , but someone types in your address *with* www., they'll simply be passed on (redirected) to the correct, canonical, version.

In step 9 there will also be a place within Webmaster Tools to tell Google which URL you want to recognize as canonical. But even with this capability we recommend truly setting your canonical URLs for the purposes of all search engines.

STEP 9: XML SITEMAP – CREATE AND SUBMIT

The final two steps wrap up our on-site work for SEO. An XML sitemap is a coded list of all URLs on your website that you would want a search engine to visit. This sitemap is not seen by your visitors, and it's not linked to from any pages of your website.

Websites with hundreds of pages or more may have a directory of xml sitemaps, broken out by category. We're not going to worry about that here. For now, you simply need to know that you'll want to create and add an xml sitemap to your website – and then submit it to search engines.

An easy way to create an xml sitemap is to use the free tool at www.xml-sitemaps.com/. You'll be able to include up to 500 pages on your sitemap with this free tool (or pay to get more). Once done, download the xml file from the tool and then upload it to your root folder. For our website this sitemap would then live at:

www.UnitedWibbles.com/sitemap.xml

Once uploaded to your website, you'll want to create a Webmaster Tool account on both Google and Bing. Within these accounts you will be able to submit your sitemap easily. In our own internal tests, testing the timing it took to index pages of a brand new website, our website with no sitemap submission took around two months to have its 10 pages indexed. But our site that we submitted an xml sitemap for was fully indexed in under two weeks.

To create your Webmaster Tools accounts go to:

Google: www.google.com/webmasters/tools

Bing/Yahoo: www.bing.com/toolbox

STEP 10: ROBOTS.TXT CREATION

The robots.txt file is the very first file a search engine looks for when it arrives at your domain. It is, quite simply, an instruction list to the search engines.

It is a simple text file that you add to your root folder. It will then reside at

www.UnitedWibbles.com/robots.txt

Though there may be some reason to get detailed in your robots.txt instructions, calling out individual bots, disallowing numerous pages on your site, etc... in most cases a robots.txt will include nothing more than the following:

```
----
User-agent: *
Disallow:
Sitemap: http://www.unitedwibbles.com/sitemap.xml
----
```

<note: the sitemap line in the robots.txt example above helps tell a search engine right away where to find the XML sitemap so you might get more of your pages indexed.

It is a best practice to include a robots.txt on every website. But if you do not have one, search engines will still find your website. So its best practice... but not critical (unless you have specific instructions for search engine bots (i.e. include/exclude directives)).

If after reading this guide you still need assistance, ThriveSearch.com offers full service online marketing services and training at every level (startup to enterprise and everything in-between). Contact for rates to help you succeed.

STEP 11: GO OFF SITE

You've completed all best practices ON your website, now it's time to focus OFF your website. Off site SEO entails link building, social media, referral generation… pretty much anything that links back to your website and generates traffic, mentions, and popularity.

You'll want to look for opportunities to build exposure and generate links. Some of the best ways to get started include:

- Create local business pages on Google and Bing
  - www.google.com/business
  - www.bingplaces.com
- Write articles and get involved in Social Bookmarking sites like Reddit, Tumblr, and StumbleUpon
- Look for business sites and directories to add your profile and website to. Depending on your business you may have only a few to choose from, or a plethora. It really depends on your market. But find every one possible and list your website.
- Engage in Social media, especially on Facebook and Twitter. Others, like Linkedin, Pinterest, Instagram, etc. depend on your business and audience.
- For best results in social media, create a blog. Attach it to your website, not somewhere else. So on our example site, our blog would live at www.UnitedWibbles.com/blog. Write new posts several times a week if possible, and then use these posts as food to feed your social media outlets (post snippets of your blog post on social sites and link back to your blog for the full content).

The reason for the blog is two-fold. Search engines continue to like fresh content. When you're constantly adding new, fresh, content your website tends to get better attention.

Another reason is keyword focus. If you have a page for blue wobbly wibbles, but you need more attention, you could find 10 – 20 different topics about blue wobbly wibbles, and create a weekly blog thread just about them.

Your ability to write new content, including optimization for the blue wobbly wibbles, will help gain your website a higher level of popularity in the eyes of Google, when someone searches for information on blue wobbly wibbles.

With your website properly optimized as I've shown you through this guide, the rest of your work relies on off-site methods. Linking, social media, and the like. But each and every one of these methods will now work far better for you because of your theme-optimized pages across your site.

One final thought… A website can be a living, growing entity. Constantly look over keywords and revise your keyword research. Add new optimized pages whenever it makes sense to do so for your business. Remember that every page of your website is like a doorway into your business, based on its theme and what your customer is searching for on a search engine.

If all you can create is 10-20 pages, okay – work with what you've got. But if those 10-20 pages can eventually turn into 100 – 200 or 1,000 – 2,000 pages, your website will be just that much more pervasive in your market, and your opportunities to show up for organic search will be that much more prolific.

ABOUT THE GUIDE AND ITS AUTHOR

Scott Orth is the founder of Thrive Business Marketing in Portland Oregon (www.ThriveSearch.com), bringing a lifetime of management and marketing experience in high-tech, hospitality, e-commerce, construction, health and nutrition, and communications.

Scott is a pioneer in SEO, and an online marketing veteran – having gotten his start in 1999 (right about the time Google was becoming known as a search engine). He worked in IT Management and ran his own online startup, while getting his B.S. in Management and Information Systems from George Fox University, and starting a family.

Having sold his business and completed his college degree, Scott then drew on his marketing and management skills to lead full-service interactive agencies, and large client-side marketing teams; building success for clients like Freightliner, Louisiana Pacific, FEI, Carrier Corporation, and hundreds of small to medium size companies; spanning many industries and business types.

With a breadth of knowledge and experience in both business-to-business and business-to-consumer online marketing, Scott has spent more than half of his career teaching and training others in the most successful ways to build, optimize, and profit from websites and web businesses. He has written dozens of articles, books, training materials, and presentations, has been published in 5 different magazines, and has created over an estimated $300 Million in new client sales during his career.

A Note from Scott:

The Indisputable Guide to SEO Success is the first in a series of guides to come. For years, I've been told that no one teaches SEO and online marketing as clearly as I do. I've purchased at least 15 other SEO books over the years. They all had one thing in common – hundreds of pages and so much unnecessary content that the actual teaching was lost.

I'm a get-to-the-point kind of guy. I've never gotten through more than 10 pages of any one of the books I purchased.

Knowing that many people share my get-to-the-point way of learning and working, I decided enough was enough. After 16 years of building success, it was time for me to show others how to do it.

I hope this guide, and others to come, prove successful in your own online marketing endeavors. If you need additional help or have questions, you can reach the Thrive team at info@thrivesearch.com or me directly at scotto@thrivesearch.com .

Additional training resources are in the works. Check our website (www.thrivesearch.com) often for updates and new materials. Or sign up for our news and tips email by texting **SEOGUIDE** to **22828** or scanning the QR Code here:

www.ingramcontent.com/pod-product-compliance
Lightning Source LLC
Chambersburg PA
CBHW041719200326
41520CB00001B/159